Wealth Strategies For Consultants: Your Guide to Financial Success

Charles H. Blum

INTRODUCTION

An Excursion with Charles H. Blum Within the universe of consultancy, there are the people who accomplish abundance as well as encapsulate the pitch of being a really effective specialist. One such illuminating presence is Charles H. Blum, a name inseparable from greatness, development, and monetary thriving in the consultancy calling.

Envision turned back the clock to meet a youthful Charles, newly confronted and energetic, as he set out on his consultancy process. Outfitted with a degree in business and a ravenous hunger for information, he entered the consultancy field with a dream that went past net revenues. His objective was clear: to help other people succeed.

Charles' initial days in consultancy reflected the difficulties looked by numerous hopefuls today. He wrestled with questions like, "How would I track down clients?" "What would it be advisable for me to charge?" and "How might I hang out in a packed market?" Yet, Charles had an exceptional quality - an unflinching obligation to conveying esteem. He put his entire being into each venture, frequently working really hard into the evening, investigating every possibility.

Through these early preliminaries, Charles revealed the primary key to his future riches: the unrelenting commitment to greatness. His clients before long perceived that when they worked with Charles H. Blum, they got something beyond an expert; they acquired a confided in accomplice in their prosperity.

As his standing developed, so did his client base. This is where Charles coincidentally found the second basic abundance procedure - the force of connections. He didn't organize for simple conditional increase; he truly associated with individuals, framing bonds that endured forever. These associations brought more activities his way as well as improved his consultancy practice vastly.

As the years passed, Charles wound up in charge of a thriving consultancy. However, what genuinely put him aside was his monetary insight. He was careful about dealing with his funds admirably, looking for guidance from specialists in charge arranging and monetary administration. This third methodology - insightful monetary stewardship - permitted him to gather abundance consistently and safely.

Charles' story isn't only one of monetary achievement; it's a demonstration of individual and expert development. He persistently extended his insight and abilities, embracing change and development. He tracked down that sensitive harmony among work and life, valuing minutes with his friends and family while having a significant effect on his clients' organizations.

Today, as we leave on this excursion through "The Rich Expert," we draw motivation from Charles H. Blum's momentous life. His story fills in as a reference point, enlightening the way to success in the consultancy scene. The rules that directed him are the very ones that we will investigate in this book - rules that can enable you to compose your own example of overcoming adversity as an expert.

Let Charles H. Blum's heritage advise us that abundance, in its most genuine structure, reaches out past financial wealth. It includes a day to day existence lived with reason, a lifelong set apart by significant effect, and a monetary eventual fate of safety and overflow.

Go along with us as we reveal the abundance techniques that will empower you to shape your own fate as an expert, similarly as Charles H. Blum did.

This presentation consolidates the tale of Charles H. Blum with the story of the book, underlining the standards he encapsulated and how they connect with the abundance procedures examined in the book.

CHAPTER 1

SETTING THE FOUNDATION

1.1 Chancing Your Consulting Focus

In the important field of consulting, changing your consulting center resembles changing your North Star. It fills in as your commanding light in an immense and Machiavellian scene, and it's the most important move toward erecting a flourishing and worthwhile consulting practice. This section investigates the meaning of characterizing your specialty and understanding how it can open the way to financial achievement.

1. Exploring the Consulting Wild: The consultancy Scene An figure of the varied and developing macrocosm of consultancy. The snares of enterprise For what reason being a handy person can obstruct your consultancy vocation. The Force of Concentration How specialization can separate you and proliferate your acquiring eventuality.

2. Feting Your consultancy: Surveying your capacities, interests, and aptitude to pinpoint your specialty. Market Investigation Exploring assiduity patterns, customer musts, and contests to fete worthwhile specialties. Contextual analyses assaying exemplifications of prostrating adversity of counsels who tracked down their specialty and flourished.

3. Statistical surveying and Request : Requesting and testing the felicity of your picked specialty through statistical surveying. customer- concentrated Approach conforming your attention to the musts and problem areas of your objective guests. Patterns and Variation Remaining lithe by ceaselessly checking assiduity drifts and conforming your concentrate in like manner.

4. Energy and Productivity: The Job of Energy Understanding how your excitement can fuel your consultancy achievement. conforming Energy and Benefit Figuring out the perfect balance where your specialty lines up with request interest. Contextual analyses in Enthusiasm Driven Achievement

Accounts of counsels who converted their interests into flourishing associations.

5. Improvement versus Specialization: The Problem Gauging the advantages and disadvantages of expanding your administrations as opposed to rehearsing. structure Versatility How improvement can defend your consultancy during request changes. spanning with Specialization The eventuality for outstanding development when you twofold down on your picked specialty.

Chancing Your consultancy focus is not just about limiting your choices; it's tied in with extending your shoes in an essential way. It's the most common way of choosing a specialty that lines up with your mastery, enthusiasm, and request interest. In this part, you will find that chancing your consultancy center is not just an introductory move toward financial achievement, but also an excursion of tone- exposure and expert growth. Your consulting career's line begins then, guided by the principles of specialization, request exploration, and a genuine passion for your chosen niche.

1.2 How To Price Your Services?

1. Seen Regards: Seen alludes to the advantages the customer gets at the cost paid for your administrations. lower charges can cause your guests to accept that you give bad quality work. At the point when you set high charges, they might think it's expensive and want something stylish. Notwithstanding, picking the right estimating model assists you with gaining the stylish appreciation for your work.

2. Request Setting : The right setting plan helps in sticking your request presence enough. This guarantees that you generally draw in the right guests for your business. You should alter your meeting charges when the business develops in view of your experience and aptitude.

3. Benefit Setting: low costs will draw in bunches of guests still would prompt financial shakiness and collapse. Going against the norm, setting lesser costs will drive your implicit guests down, bringing about a business mischance over the long haul. Accordingly, picking the right system will bring likely guests and let you stay on the productivity side.

4. Customer Supposition: At the point when you charge an inordinate cost, guests anticipate ultra expensive administrations from you. On the other hand, when you set low costs, they've lower hypotheticals from you. This is on the grounds that, with a low valuing plan, they illustrate to you that it does not match standard quality. To this end you should bring a typical cost matching your customer's hypotheticals. And likewise does equity to your business. Keep pursuing to comprehend the kinds of consultancy valuing procedures, and subsequently find the most effective way to pick the stylish assessing system for your consultancy establishment.

1.3 Creating Your Consulting Business Plan

In the world of consulting, a well-crafted business plan serves as your roadmap to success. This chapter explores the essential steps and strategies for creating a comprehensive consulting business plan that not only charts your course but also maximizes your potential for financial prosperity.

1.3.1 The Outline of Progress

•**The Job of a Marketable strategy:** Understanding how a marketable strategy characterizes your consultancy practice's motivation, objectives, and procedures.

•**The Force of Vision:** How an unmistakable and convincing vision explanation can rouse and direct your consultancy.

•**Laying out Shrewd Objectives:** Creating explicit, quantifiable, reachable, significant, and time-bound objectives to drive your prosperity.

1.3.2 Market Examination and Exploration

•**The consultancy Scene:** Dissecting the cutthroat scene and market patterns.

•**Client Profiles:** Recognizing and understanding your objective clients' requirements, inclinations, and trouble spots.

•**Contender Examination:** Surveying the qualities and shortcomings of rivals in your specialty.

1.3.3 Characterizing Your Administrations and Incentive

•**Administration Contributions:** Specifying the consultancy administrations you'll give and their interesting selling focuses.

•**Offer:** Imparting the unmistakable worth you bring to your clients and how it separates you.

•**Estimating Methodologies:** Deciding your valuing structure in light of your administrations and market situating.

1.3.4 Showcasing and Client Obtaining

•**Showcasing Systems:** Illustrating the promoting channels and strategies you'll utilize to arrive at your main interest group.

Deals Techniques: Planning your business approach and client procurement process.

•**Building Your Image:** Procedures for building and advancing areas of strength for a brand.

1.3.5 Monetary Projections and Planning

•**Monetary Conjecture:** Projecting your pay, costs, and productivity over a characterized period.

•**Planning**: Making a financial plan to guarantee you distribute assets successfully and oversee income.

•**Risk Appraisal:** Recognizing expected monetary dangers and creating moderation procedures.

1.3.6 Tasks and Group Design

•**Functional Arrangement:** Portraying the everyday activities of your consultancy, including client the board, project conveyance, and organization.

•**Group Construction:** Characterizing the jobs and obligations of your colleagues, if pertinent.

•**Adaptability:** Procedures for scaling your consultancy as it develops.

1.3.7 Execution and Checking

•**Move Steps:** Illustrating the substantial advances you'll initiate to carry out your strategy.

•**Key Execution Markers (KPIs):** Characterizing the measurements and achievements you'll screen to keep tabs on your development.

•**Nonstop Improvement:** The significance of auditing and modifying your marketable strategy as your consultancy advances.

CHAPTER 2

ATTRACTING CLIENTS AND PROJECTS

2.1 Promoting Your Consulting Services

Advancing your consultancy administrations really is the extension between your aptitude and your clients. This part investigates the craftsmanship and study of advertising and advancement in the consultancy scene, outfitting you with the systems to draw in clients, fabricate your standing, and eventually, accomplish monetary thriving.

2.1.2 The Consultancy Brand

Brand Personality: Making areas of strength for a paramount brand character that mirrors your skill and values.

Brand Consistency: Keeping up with consistency across the entirety of your showcasing materials, online presence, and client associations.

Brand Trust: Building entrust with your crowd through reliable conveyance of significant worth and commitments.

2.1.3 Main Interest Group And Division

Distinguishing Your Optimal Clients: Characterizing your interest group in light of their necessities, qualities, and socioeconomics.

Client Division: Fitting your advertising messages and ways to deal with explicit client fragments.

Personal Advancement: Making itemized client personas to all the more likely get it and interface with your crowd.

2.1.4 Computerized Presence and Internet Promoting

Site Streamlining: Guaranteeing your site is a strong showcasing device, simple to explore, and Website design enhancement cordial.

Content Showcasing: Making significant, applicable, and steady satisfaction to lay out experts in your specialty.

Web-based Entertainment Methodology: Utilizing online entertainment stages to interface with clients, share experiences, and advance your administrations.

2.1.5 Thought Authority and Content Creation

Thought Initiative: Securing yourself as an industry thoroughly considered pioneer wise substance.

Content Sorts: Investigating different substance designs, like web journals, articles, whitepapers, recordings, and digital broadcasts.

Content Conveyance: Decisively sharing your substance through various channels to contact a more extensive crowd.

2.1.5 Systems administration and Relationship Building

Organizing Methodologies: Creating organizing plans to interface with peers, possible clients, and industry powerhouses.

Building Veritable Connections: The significance of earnestness, trust, and common help in systems administration.

Reference Organizations: Investigating cooperation valuable open doors with different experts and organizations.

2.1.6 Client Tributes and Contextual analyses

Bridling Social Evidence: The force of client tributes and examples of overcoming adversity in building believability.

Contextual investigation Improvement: How to make convincing contextual analyses that grandstand your aptitude and results.

Consent and Protection: Guaranteeing you have the essential authorizations to utilize client tributes and contextual investigations.

2.1.7 Estimating and Investigating Showcasing Achievement

Key Measurements: Distinguishing and following the key execution pointers (KPIs) of your showcasing endeavors.

Investigation Devices: Using examination instruments to acquire experiences into the adequacy of your showcasing efforts.

Persistent Improvement: Utilizing information to refine your promoting procedures and amplify your return for capital invested.

Advancing your consultancy administrations isn't just about promoting; it's tied in with building a brand, interfacing with your crowd, and conveying esteem. This furnishes you with the instruments and experiences to hoist your promoting endeavors and draw in clients who value your skill. By dominating the procedures illustrated here, you'll be well en route to accomplishing monetary success as a specialist.

2.2   Building A Portfolio

Building a portfolio is similar to building a house. You need a plan that you will be content with and that addresses your family's issues. You'll have to utilize a wide assortment of materials. Furthermore, what counts isn't simply the nature of those materials yet additionally the way in which they cooperate.

2.3 Networking And Building Relationships

2.3.1 Joint efforts and Organizations

Vital Unions: The section talks about the advantages of framing associations and partnerships with different experts or organizations.

Shared benefit Joint efforts: Systems for recognizing commonly advantageous cooperation and amazing open doors.

Keeping up with Cooperative Connections: How to support and fortify associations over the long run.

2.3.2 Estimating Systems administration Achievement

Key Execution Pointers (KPIs): Distinguishing and following measurements, like the quantity of new associations, references, or fruitful associations.

Assessing Connections: Systems for occasionally surveying the quality and worth of your organization associations.

Constant Improvement: Utilizing information and criticism to refine your systems administration methodology for improved results.

2.3.3 Winning Projects With Effective Proposals

In the unique universe of consultancy, getting projects is the soul of your training. It's the scaffold between your aptitude and client needs, and the way to monetary success. The specialty of creating powerful recommendations is the expert's distinct advantage. It's not just about submitting archives; about making powerful stories to resonate with clients, separate you from contenders, and at last win projects.

1.The Proposition as an Impetus

Proposition Importance: This part highlights the basic job of recommendations as the need might arise.

The Influential ability: The investigation starts by featuring that compelling recommendations are convincing devices that can separate you from contenders.

2. Creating a Proposition Methodology

Characterizing Proposition Targets: Defining clear objectives for your recommendations, whether it's getting another venture or growing a current client relationship.

Designated Proposition: Adjusting your recommendations to address the particular necessities and trouble spots of your clients.

Proposition Arranging: Methodologies for orderly and effective proposition improvement, from exploration to definite accommodation.

3. The Life systems of a Triumphant Proposition

Construction and Configuration: The section investigates the ideal design and organization of a proposition, including introductory letters, chief synopses, and nitty gritty undertaking plans.

- **Client-Focused Approach:** The significance of fitting your proposition to feature how your consultancy administrations will straightforwardly help the client.

- **Clear and Succinct Language:** Techniques for conveying complex thoughts and arrangements in clear, peruser amicable language.

4. Displaying Your Ability

Exhibiting Skill: The investigation dives into procedures for displaying your capabilities, experience, and past victories.

Contextual Investigations and Tributes: Utilizing contextual analyses and client tributes to give certifiable proof of your abilities.

Thought Initiative: Situating yourself as an idea chief in your proposition by offering one of a kind bits of knowledge and creative arrangements.

5. Tending to Client Concerns

Distinguishing Client Concerns: Techniques for expecting and tending to potential client protests or inquiries in your proposition.

Risk Relief: Showing how you'll oversee dangers and difficulties related with the proposed project.

Open Correspondence: The significance of empowering client criticism and inquiries during the proposition audit process.

6. Estimating and Incentive

Estimating Procedures: The section talks about different evaluating models, from hourly rates to project-based expenses, and how to adjust them to your incentive.

Esteem Based Evaluating: Investigating the idea of significant worth based estimating and how to convey the worth you give in your proposition.

Clear Expense Breakdowns: Giving straightforward expense breakdowns to assist clients with figuring out the speculation and advantages of your administrations.

7. The Proposition Survey Interaction

Proposition Accommodation: Techniques for presenting your proposition expertly and it are incorporated to guarantee every single required material.

Client Coordinated effort: The significance of open and cooperative correspondence with clients during the proposition survey.

Post-Proposition Follow-Up: How to follow up successfully after proposition accommodation to resolve any leftover various forms of feedback.

CHAPTER 3

EXCELLING IN YOUR CONSULTANCY

3.1 Delivering Exceptional Consulting

In the unique universe of consultancy, getting projects is the soul of your training. It's the scaffold between your aptitude and client needs, and the way to monetary success. The specialty of creating powerful recommendations is the expert's distinct advantage. It's not just about submitting archives; about making powerful stories to resonate with clients, separate you from contenders, and at last win projects.

This thorough aide will investigate the methodologies, strategies, and best practices that can change your proposition into incredible assets for progress. From setting clear targets to tending to client concerns and displaying your skill, we will dig profound into the components that make up a triumphant proposition.

3.1.1 The Proposition as an Impetus

Proposition Importance: This part highlights the basic job of recommendations as the need might arise.

The Influential ability: The investigation starts by featuring that compelling recommendations are convincing devices that can separate you from contenders.

3.1.2 Creating a Proposition Methodology

Characterizing Proposition Targets: Defining clear objectives for your recommendations, whether it's getting another venture or growing a current client relationship.

Designated Proposition: Adjusting your recommendations to address the particular necessities and trouble spots of your clients.

Proposition Arranging: Methodologies for orderly and effective proposition improvement, from exploration to definite accommodation.

The Life systems of a Triumphant Proposition

Construction and Configuration: The section investigates the ideal design and organization of a proposition, including introductory letters, chief synopses, and nitty gritty undertaking plans.

Client-Focused Approach: The significance of fitting your proposition to feature how your consultancy administrations will straightforwardly help the client.

Clear and Succinct Language: Techniques for conveying complex thoughts and arrangements in clear, peruser amicable language.

3.1.3 Displaying Your Ability

Exhibiting Skill: The investigation dives into procedures for displaying your capabilities, experience, and past victories.

Contextual investigations and Tributes: Utilizing contextual analyses and client tributes to give certifiable proof of your abilities.

Thought Initiative: Situating yourself as an idea chief in your proposition by offering one of a kind bits of knowledge and creative arrangements.

3.1.4 Tending to Client Concerns

Distinguishing Client Concerns: Techniques for expecting and tending to potential client protests or inquiries in your proposition.

Risk Relief: Showing how you'll oversee dangers and difficulties related with the proposed project.

Open Correspondence: The significance of empowering client criticism and inquiries during the proposition audit process.

3.1.5 Estimating and Incentive

Estimating Procedures: The section talks about different evaluating models, from hourly rates to project-based expenses, and how to adjust them to your incentive.

Esteem Based Evaluating: Investigating the idea of significant worth based estimating and how to convey the worth you give in your proposition.

Clear Expense Breakdowns: Giving straightforward expense breakdowns to assist clients with figuring out the speculation and advantages of your administrations.

3.1.6 The Proposition Survey Interaction

Proposition Accommodation: Techniques for presenting your proposition expertly and it are incorporated to guarantee every single required material.

Client Coordinated effort: The significance of open and cooperative correspondence with clients during the proposition survey.

Post-Proposition Follow-Up: How to follow up successfully after proposition accommodation to resolve any leftover various forms of feedback.

3.2   MANAGING   CLIENTS EXPECTATIONS

Overseeing client assumptions is a basic expertise in consultancy. It includes adjusting what clients expect with what you can practically convey, guaranteeing straightforwardness, and keeping up with open correspondence all through the consultancy commitment. Here is an exhaustive aide on the best way to really oversee client assumptions:

3.2.1 Introductory Meeting and Revelation Stage

Listen Effectively: Start by effectively paying attention to your client's necessities, objectives, and worries during the underlying meeting.

Seek clarification on pressing issues: Urge clients to plainly express their assumptions and wanted results.

Set Practical Assumptions: In the event that you anticipate any difficulties or restrictions in measuring up to their assumptions, impart them genuinely at this stage.

Instruct Clients: Offer bits of knowledge into the consultancy system and what they can sensibly anticipate during each period of the commitment.

3.2.2 Characterize Venture Degree

Scope Definition: Obviously characterize the extent of the task, including expectations, courses of events, and any likely restrictions.

Scope Understanding: Guarantee both you and the client settle on the task's degree recorded as a hard copy through a proper understanding or agreement.

Archive Changes: Assuming there are any degree changes during the undertaking, report them obviously and talk about the possible effect on courses of events and expenses with the client.

3.2.3 Correspondence and Straightforwardness

Normal Updates: Keep up with reliable and straightforward correspondence with clients all through the task. Give normal updates on progress, difficulties, and achievements.

Straightforwardness in Issues: Assuming surprising issues emerge that could influence the task, illuminate the client right away. Talk about expected arrangements and their suggestions.

Oversee Assumptions Proactively: In the event that there are any progressions in the task's timetable or degree, illuminate the client immediately and make sense of the explanations for the changes.

3.2.4 Set Reasonable Courses of events

Reasonable Cutoff times: Guarantee that project courses of events are sensible and reachable in view of the extent of work and accessible assets.

Cushion for Unexpected Postponements: Incorporate a cradle for unanticipated deferrals or difficulties that might emerge during the undertaking.

3.2.5 Oversee Dangers Successfully

Risk Appraisal: Recognize potential dangers that could influence the undertaking of a positive outcome. Foster gamble moderation procedures and impart them to the client.

Emergency courses of action: Have alternate courses of action set up for addressing surprising difficulties to limit their effect on the undertaking.

3.2.6 Client Instruction

Instruct on Interaction: Assist clients with understanding the consultancy system, including its stages, procedures, and the time expected for each stage.

Sensible Results: Instruct clients about what is feasible inside the limitations of their undertaking, financial plan, and time period.

3.2.7 Keep a Positive Relationship

Develop Trust: Fabricate areas of strength for an of trust with the client through incredible skill, dependability, and reliably following through on guarantees.

Address Concerns: On the off chance that a client communicates concerns or disappointment, address them immediately and expertly. Look for commonly pleasant arrangements.

3.2.8 Look for Criticism

Criticism Circles: Lay out input systems that permit clients to share their contemplations, concerns, and ideas all through the venture.

Consistent Improvement: Use client criticism as a chance for ceaseless improvement in your consultancy practice.

3.2.9 Last Survey and Assessment

Survey Objectives: During the venture conclusion, return to the underlying objectives and targets to evaluate how well they were met.

Illustrations Learned: Direct examples learned meeting with the client to distinguish regions for development and assemble bits of knowledge for future ventures.

Successfully overseeing client assumptions is a continuous cycle that requires clear correspondence, straightforwardness, and a pledge to conveying esteem. By following these techniques and keeping a client-focused approach, experts can construct trust, upgrade client fulfillment, and guarantee fruitful consultancy commitment.

3.3 HANDLING CHALLENGING CLIENTS AND SITUATIONS

3.3.1 Figure out Your Clients

The initial step to deal with a troublesome client or circumstance is to attempt to grasp their viewpoint, requirements, and objectives. You can utilize undivided attention, sympathy, and questions that could go either way to assemble compatibility and entrust with your client and to distinguish their assets and difficulties. You can likewise utilize social capability, variety mindfulness, and hostile to harsh practice to regard and esteem your client's character, foundation, and encounters. By understanding your client, you can keep away from presumptions, generalizations, and decisions that might obstruct your relationship and administration conveyance.

Utilizing effectively tuning in and exhibiting sympathy to comprehend the client's viewpoint as well as understanding that while the conduct the client showcases might be troublesome, it is much of the time brought about by basic issues connected with psychological maladjustment, injury or other brokenness. Whenever I zeroed in on the arrangements and not the broken conduct shown by the client, it permitted me to be more successful in giving them the administrations expected to help them.

3.3.2 Put down Stopping points And Assumptions

Another significant step is to define clear and reasonable limits and assumptions with your client and yourself. You can utilize an agreement or consent to frame the jobs, obligations, and objectives of your social work mediation and to explain the restrictions of your contribution and accessibility. You can likewise utilize confident correspondence, criticism, and support to deal with your client's way of behaving and assumptions and to resolve any issues or clashes that might emerge.

I absolutely concur! Making limits and setting assumptions in the start of the treatment cycle is fundamental! The patient understands what they really should anticipate from their meetings and how to best use them. Defining these limits likewise assists work with believing between the patient and supplier, which is a critical figure giving fruitful treatment.

3.3.3 Use Proof based Intercessions

A third step is to utilize proof based intercessions that are shown to be compelling and proper for your client and circumstance. You can utilize different models, structures, and speculations of social work practice to direct your appraisal, arranging, execution, and assessment of your intercession.

Proof based intercessions are a compelling apparatus for social specialists while working with troublesome clients. Proof based intercessions are intended to decrease trouble, increment prosperity, and advance positive results. They depend on research that has been led throughout the long term and plan to give proof based answers for complex issues. Proof based mediations can likewise be utilized to assist social specialists with fostering a thorough arrangement for their clients, as well as help them in grasping the intricacies of their clients' circumstances. By exploring and executing proof based mediations, social laborers can turn out to be more powerful in their training and give improved results to their clients.

3.3.4 Look for Interview And Backing

A fourth step is to look for discussion and backing from your partners, managers, tutors, or different experts when you face a troublesome client or circumstance. You can utilize peer backing, oversight, or coaching to talk about your difficulties, look for input, gain from others' encounters, and upgrade your abilities and information. You can likewise utilize references, coordinated effort, or promotion to get to extra assets, administrations, or backing for your client or yourself. For instance, you can allude your client to a particular office, team up with a multidisciplinary group, or supporter for foundational change contingent upon your client's necessities and objectives.

1) When the circumstance surpasses your skill or limit: Consider talking with experienced partners or managers in the event that you have a dubious outlook on the best way to deal with a complicated issue.

2) When the client's necessities are past your ongoing preparation: On the off chance that you want extra assets or abilities to address a client's issues, go to other people who might have more skill nearby.

3)When intercessions come up short: Think about elective techniques on the off chance that a mediation has not been fruitful, or on the other hand assuming there is no proof accessible to help further utilization of that methodology.

4)When joint effort is required: Working with different experts can open up additional opportunities for creating clever fixes and medicines that benefit the client.

3.3.5. Reflect And Learn

A last step is to reflect and gain from your encounters of dealing with troublesome clients and circumstances. You can utilize reflection, assessment, or criticism to analyze your considerations, sentiments, activities, and results and to distinguish your assets and regions for development. You can likewise utilize learning, proficient turn of events, or preparing to refresh your insight, abilities, and skills and to address any holes or difficulties in your training. By reflecting and learning, you can improve your mindfulness, certainty, and viability as a social laborer.

3.4 GROWING YOUR CONSULTING BUSINESS

Growing a consultancy business requires an essential methodology that includes customer carrying, notoriety structure, extending administrations, and effective tasks. There's a total primer for help you with getting your consultancy business

1. Characterize Your Specialty: Distinguish a particular specialty or assiduity where you can offer profound skill and stick out. Statistical surveying Direct ferocious statistical surveying to figure out the musts, difficulties, and open doors inside your picked specialty.

2. Construct Areas of strength for a complete: Marking Put coffers into complete marking, including a satisfying totem, point, and showcasing accouterments . intriguing incitement Obviously convey what separates your consultancy administrations from contenders.

3. Foster a Strong Internet grounded: Presence Site Enhancement Guarantee Your point is easy to understand, protean, responsive, and better for web indicators(Web optimization). Content Promoting Make and offer important material, for illustration, blog entries, whitepapers, and online classes, to parade your capability.

4. Systems administration and Relationship structure: Go to Assiduity Occasions Take part in meetings, shops, and systems administration occasions to associate with possible guests and companions. Web grounded Systems administration share in web- grounded gatherings, virtual entertainment gatherings, and stages like LinkedIn to extend your association.

5. Customer Carrying Customer: References appetite fulfilled guests to allude your administrations to other people. Cold Effort Foster a designated outreach fashion to move toward implicit guests directly, displaying how your administrations can attack their enterprises.

6. Offer A Compass Of Administrations: Consider growing your administration benefactions to take special care of a more expansive compass of customer requirements. Strategically pitching Elevate complementary administrations to bring guests to proliferation income from every customer relationship.

7. Influence Innovation Project: The directors Instruments Use design the board and common trouble accouterments to smooth out conditioning and further develop customer correspondence. robotization Computerize routine errands, for illustration, arrangement planning and invoicing, to save time for vital exercises.

8. Put Coffers Into Complete: Turn of events harmonious literacy Remain refreshed with assiduity patterns and marches through workrooms, courses, and instruments.

Mentorship: Look for mentorship from educated specialists who can give direction and bits of knowledge.

9. Oversee finances Wisely: Make a fiscal plan that designates means for showcasing, invention, and development drives. Monetary Investigation routinely anatomizes your financial donation to fete regions for development.

10. Customer conservation: Surpass hypotheticals Reliably convey uncommon backing to hold being guests and encourage long haul connections. Ordinary Enrollments Timetable occasional enrollments with guests to survey their advancing musts and proposition redundant worth.

11. Measure crucial measures crucial prosecution Pointers(KPIs): Characterize and follow KPIs connected with customer carrying, income development, and customer fulfillment. Information Driven Choices Use information examination to pursue informed choices and change your development procedures meetly.

12. Spanning Your Business: Consider employing redundant specialists or care staff. Diversifying or Permitting probe choices like diversifying or authorizing your consultancy model to extend provincially or astronomically.

13. Convey Greatness thickness: Keep a standing for conveying predictable, great issues to guests. customer Tribute's appetite fulfilled guests to give paeans that can be displayed on your point and showcasing accouterments .

14. Vital hookups Associations: Structure vital associations with different associations or experts that condense your administrations. Reference Arrangements Lay out reference concurrences with non-contending experts who can allude guests to you.

15. Survey and Acclimate: Intermittent Assessment constantly estimates your development procedures, changes your methodology depending on the situation, and stays patient to changing profitable situations. Growing a consultancy business is an important excursion that requires a blend of skill, promoting, customer connections, and functional proficiency. By executing these ways and keeping a customer- concentrated approach, you can constantly extend your consultancy practice and make long haul progress.

CHAPTER 4

FINANCIAL SUCCESS

4.1. Managing Your Finances

Financial management is essential for the sustained growth and prosperity of an organization. It entails organizing, managing, controlling, and keeping an eye on your financial resources in order to achieve your organization's goals. You may accept your money, the executives are confused and amazing, but the following eight financial management tips will help you regain control.

Financial management needs to be supported in your long-term planning and integrated into your organization's main cycles. It could help you take advantage of the resources you have more effectively, fulfill your partner commitments, gain the upper hand, and prepare for long-term stability.

Lack of financial management skills can lead to a wide range of difficulties, such as underfunding your group and failing to pay representatives for their time. Here are some financial management tricks and suggestions from experts to make sure you have the best financial plan in place.

1. Reduce Your Expenses: One of the most important things to stay going is to keep your uses low. Consider the quality quantity carefully when calculating operational costs. Just purchase the items that are essential for your work; avoid consuming anything extra.

The travel sector is one that needs to be carefully examined. Travel may be very expensive, especially if you have to spend the nights in hotels or work from another country. To save money, consider using video conferencing technology to arrange virtual meetings with clients instead of traveling to in-person events.

2. Make plans for expansion: As your company grows, you'll most likely need to hire more employees and invest in new hardware and office space. Make sure you have a plan in place for how you will pay for these expenses. Consider the price of marketing planning as well as the cost of developing marketing practices. Expecting future expenses and planning will help to ensure that your organization does not run into financial difficulties in the near future. Similarly, and more importantly, it prevents financial concerns from stifling your company's growth. This is where effective financial management comes in - without it, unexpected expenses might catch you off guard and delay your progress.

For example, rather than burning through cash on essential charges like finance or supplies, the board can keep firms waiting for seller installments or deferred client installments.

When it comes to saving money, it is critical to seek professional advice in order to make informed decisions. Conduct the essential research and invest in products that may provide you with good profits in the long run.

The best method to ensure that your efforts are profitable is to consult with a competent financial advisor. Your advisor can assist you in developing a money-growth strategy that meets your present and future needs. Regardless of the fact that their administrations may have some important drawbacks, saving money wisely might save you time and money in the long run.

3. Track cash flow daily: Numerous businesses don't have a suitable income the board framework set up, leading to numerous unneeded complications. At a given point or another, most consulting companies finish handling monetary challenges brought about by improper administration of their money. Frequently it is past due to steer away from major harms when they at long last admit they ought to have been more proactive with their finances.

For this reason it's vital to routinely screen your organization's money status (no less than one time per week). It is suggested that you need to attempt an online application to monitor all approaching and active cash gradually. Thus, you can constantly respond promptly at whatever point new challenges develop.

Notwithstanding income from the board, it is crucial to guarantee that your organization has a great monetary administration framework set up. It ought to encompass planning, invoicing, debt claims, creditor liability, and records payable cycles. Taking on these apparatuses will assist you with trying not to burn through cash superfluously and further improve client relations. Monitoring these errands day to day might be laborious so explore computerizing them utilizing a bookkeeping programming bundle or an ERP framework.

4. Set realistic budgets: Many organizations disregard the amount it will cost to follow through on an effort or program. On the off chance that you don't have a thought of your genuine expenses, you can either finish or underbid undertakings or projects - bringing up an insufficient spending plan. An appealing monetary and the executives accounts framework implies creating practical financial plans that appropriately integrate cash to handle surprising charges and to ensure you're not left short at month-end.

It additionally implies ensuring vendors are paid on schedule, so they keep supplying top notch support to your firm. This is termed income to the executives, which is similarly all about as vital as effective monetary administration yet usually overlooked by entrepreneurs.

The most ideal strategy to outline a sensible spending plan is to keep nitty gritty records of every one of your utilizations, so you know precisely how much cash it costs to maintain your organization every month. Then, at that point, use those data to develop sensible objectives while offering assignments or initiatives. Assuming there's any additional money left over at month-end, place that in reserve funds or apply it to squaring away obligation.

Join to attempt the top cost tracker program and constantly build sensible spending plans for your organization.

5. Invest in yourself: To stay informed of the opposition, you should keep steady over the most recent news and patterns. It's vital to constantly put resources into yourself and your business. This implies going to courses, studios, and other preparation occasions that can aid you with working on your talents and information. It's equally worth investigating different approaches you can put cash into your organization. For instance, in the event that you have a site, it very well may merit spending resources into an excellent website composition. On the off chance that you're running a web based business website, it could pay off to devote resources into a RapidSSL declaration. You likewise need to put resources into a dependable web facilitating for Online business for a superior webpage speed, execution and security.

Notwithstanding self-training, it's crucial to appreciate how to actually deal with your business' monetary records. In the event that you don't know where your cash is going, it may very well be difficult to halt unnecessary spending before you're in a problematic circumstance. Viable monetary administration also goes out to knowing techniques of further increasing income, for example, having a particular measure of stores set aside that can assist you with getting by assuming organization dials back out of the blue.

6. Diversify your income sources: Expanding your pay sources is a fantastic way for lowering your gamble on the off chance that one of your fundamental wellsprings of cash evaporates. By having numerous income streams, you'll be less subject to any one form of revenue and, in this fashion, less inclined to confront monetary problems.

7. Stay disciplined: As an entrepreneur, you should hone in on expanding your income while controlling expenses. With that in mind, it's vital to be conservative with regards to your spending — while ensuring you save sufficient money for prospective later use. Know about how money goes via your corporation to discover what locations are depleting cash and where income needs to get. Also, remember about receivables (on the off chance that you do, at last, you could wind up with horrible responsibilities).

Everything integrates back with a crucial monetary rule: There must be more cash coming in than going out. In any case, you risk running out of funds – and finally running bankrupt.

Ensure your ledgers typically show positive adjusts; on the off chance that they don't, do whatever it takes to make them so at the earliest opportunity! You may oversee what you measure.

8. Invest your money wisely: When it comes to investing your money, it's critical to seek comprehensive advice in order to make informed decisions. Do the essential research and invest in specifics that will potentially provide you with good returns in the long run.The most efficient strategy to ensure that your gambling profits are of high quality is to consult with an expert financial advisor. Your companion can assist you in developing a growth strategy that will meet your present and future needs. Regardless of the fact that their administrations may entail some major risks, putting money away wisely might set aside your time and cash in later times.

9. Handle your responsibilities wisely: It's prudent to manage your obligations well in order to decrease the amount of interest you pay on outstanding balances. Use a Visa Mini-computer or to determine the amount you're paying in interest each time and try to take care of as much of your obligation as possible. Keep in mind that catching scores might have a negative impact on the board's profits because it takes money that could be provided more profitably elsewhere.To properly manage your obligation, make sure you keep an eye out for any unusual balances. Know when your credit limit will be reached so that you can avoid unnecessary expenditures.

4.2 NAVIGATING LEGAL AND DUTY CONSIDERATIONS

Exploring legit and burden contemplations is an essential part of maintaining a consultancy business. rightly tending to these issues can help you with working legitimately, limit charge arrears, and guard your business. Beginning a consultancy establishment is an extraordinary system for stretching out and offering administrations under your own image.

Nonetheless, you'll have to suppose about four legal issues from the beginning of your firm limitations in your work contract.

4.2.1 Enrolling your brand name

Drafting a client understanding that guarantees you get compensatedSettling on a business structure. Every one of these issues are tended to. so you can begin your consultancy establishment on the right foot.

4.2.2 Limitations in Your Business Agreement

It's essential to guarantee that you won't break the restriction of exchange commitments in your current or formerly work contracts. Assuming you're a worker or design worker of a current establishment, the agreement will presumably say that you can't move toward being guests; and can't set up a contending business.

Limitations can apply for quite a long time or they can extend on for a really long time. In this way, figuring out what limitations apply is critical. It's indeed really smart to check once business contracts. In any case, you risk piercing your old agreement. This could indicate that your old establishment can seek after you in court. The court might grant detriment against you, or request you to quit setting up the firm.

4.2.3 Enlisting your Brand name

Applying for an exchange imprint ought to be a right on time schedule thing. Enrolling an exchange mark permits you to only use the brand name you decided for your consultancy firm.Try not to get confused between enlisting a business name and enrolling in an exchange mark.

Enlisting a business name simply implies that the Australian Business Register(ABR) presently has your business name on a register. It doesn't indicate that you can help different associations from exercising commodities with a truly similar or similar name.

Then again, enlisting an exchange mark implies that you can keep different associations from exercising commodities similar or analogous to an exchange imprint or   hallmark, which is critical if you need to fabricate areas of strength for.

4.2.4 Drafting a Client Understanding that Guarantees

You get compensated when your coming schedule is to get a truly important drafted client understanding for your consultancy establishment which sets out the consultancy administrations you will give; how and when your guests pay you; and what moves you might initiate in the event that your guests neglect pay. likewise address protected ideas;

Protected innovation

On the off chance that you make reports or other material for your guests, your client arranges requirements to address defended inventions(IP). Any material you use over and over, similar to a report format, ought to no way be doled out to a client. The client understanding ought to express that you permit the client to use any reports you give, yet that you don't dole out the IP in the base format.

You depend on your client to give you entrance to the data. You should have the option to offer the types of backing and on time. This ought to be drafted into the client's understanding under a' guarantees' condition, where your client vows to furnish you with data and concurrence to your sensible conjurations as soon as possible.

The promises statement also, at that point, should be followed up by a custom fitted end condition. Urgently, the end statement ought to frame that in the event that the relationship separates, you keep the option to end the arrangement. For case, on the off chance that the client hasn't given data in an ideal style, leaving you unfit to express what you guaranteed. Usually this is a final retreat situation, yet you must reserve the honor to end when the client is to blame.

- **Purchaser Certifications**

Regardless of whether you're offering types of backing to associations, numerous guests might be good to depend on if the buyer ensures set out in the Australian customer Regulation(upper leg tendon). For your consultancy establishment, this implies that you should furnish your consultancy administrations with due care and capability. You should likewise guarantee that the administrations are good for the reason you publicize. On the off chance that your administrations have a minor or significant disappointment, the client might be good for a reduction. On the other hand, you might have tore- play out the administrations.

- **Settling on a Business Construction**

At long last, you ought to conclude which business design will suit your objects. It's smarter to maintain the business as an association in the event that you will look for outside speculation.

An association likewise restricts your trouble. Just association resources can be employed to pay association scores. Debt holders will not have the option to guarantee your own resources. Again, being a sole dealer implies you are by and by at trouble to pay the business's obligations.

Getting the legal considerations right at the launch lets you grow your consulting establishment with confidence. differently, you may find your consultancy establishment shut down by a former employer, or enter difficulties with guests that could have been avoided.

4.3 Building Your Wealth

Building wealth is a long- term fiscal thing that requires careful planning, chastened saving and investing, and smart fiscal opinions. Then is a comprehensive companion on how to make and grow your wealth over timeFormalizing a list of fiscal pretensions can help. Setting fiscal pretensions may help you prioritize. They 're a way of giving you a clear idea of why you 're saving your hard- earned plutocrat. "

4.3.1. Set Clear Financial Goals

Define Your pretensions: easily outline your fiscal objectives, whether it's saving for withdrawal, buying a home, or funding your children's education. Prioritize pretensions: Determine which pretensions are most important and prioritize them grounded on your current fiscal situation.

4.3.2. Produce a Budget

Track Your Charges: Dissect your yearly spending to understand where your plutocrat goes.

Establishing a Budget: Produce a realistic budget that allocates a portion of your income toward savings and investments.

Emergency Fund: Prioritize erecting an emergency fund that covers at least three to six months' worth of living charges.

4.3.3. Save and Invest Wisely

Automate Savings: Set up automatic transfers to savings or investment accounts to insure harmonious contributions.

Diversify Investments: Diversify your investment portfolio across colorful asset classes, similar as stocks, bonds, real estate, and indispensable investments.

Risk Tolerance: Assess your threat forbearance and choose investments that align with your threat profile.

Invest for the Long Term: Stay invested for the long term to profit from compounding returns.

4.3.4. Manage Debt

Pay Off High- Interest Debt: Prioritize paying out high- interest debts, similar as credit card balances, to reduce interest payments.

Debt connection: Consider consolidating or refinancing debts to lower interest rates and streamline repayments.

Responsible Use of Credit: Use credit responsibly and avoid accumulating gratuitous debt.

4.3.5. Increase Your Income Career Development

Side Hustles: Explore openings for fresh income through side businesses or freelance work.

Negotiate Compensation: Negotiate for competitive compensation and benefits in your job or freelance contracts.

6. Maximize Tax Efficiency

Tax-advantaged: Accounts contribute to duty-advantaged withdrawal accounts like 401(k) s, IRAs, or HSAs to lower your duty liability and increase savings.

Tax Planning: Strategically plan your investments and income to minimize duty obligations.

Consult a Tax Professional: Work with a duty counsel to optimize your duty strategy.

4.3.7 Continuously Educate Yourself For Financial knowledge

Investment Knowledge: Learn about different investment options and strategies to make informed decisions. Stay informed about particular finance and investment principles.

Seek Professional Advice: Consult fiscal counsels or experts when necessary, especially for complex fiscal matters.

4.3.8. Estate Planning

Will and Estate Plan: Produce a will and an estate plan to insure your means are distributed according to your wishes.

Beneficiary Designations: Review and update device designations on fiscal accounts and insurance programs.

4.3.9. Charitable Giving

Philanthropy considers charitable paying as part of your fiscal plan, both for the benefit of causes you support and implicit duty advantages.

4.3.10. Review and Adjust Regular Assessment

Periodically review your fiscal pretensions, investments, and budget to make necessary adjustments. Be conservative of life affectation as your income increases, and continue to save and invest.

4.3.11. Stay Disciplined and Patient

Long- Term Perspective: Building wealth takes time; avoid impulsive opinions and stay married to your fiscal goals.

4.3.12. Seek fiscal Independence

Financial Independence: Aim for fiscal independence where your unresistant income covers your living charges, furnishing you with further inflexibility and freedom.

CHAPTER 5

PERSONAL AND PROFESSIONAL GROWTH

5.1 Nonstop Acquiring And Expertise Improvement

Nonstop abilities improvement alludes to the continuous course of obtaining new abilities or working on existing ones.

Constant mastering and expertise improvement are fundamental viewpoints for consultancy experts to flourish in a profoundly cutthroat and dynamic industry. In the present quickly changing business scene, the capacity to adjust, update information, and upgrade abilities is significant for giving top notch consultancy administrations. This examination will dig into the meaning of nonstop acquiring and expertise advancement in consultancy benefits and give a few vital procedures to execute them successfully.

5.1.1. Significances of Constant Acquiring and Ability Improvement:

1. Remaining Refreshed: Constant learning guarantees that specialists keep up to date with the most recent industry patterns, market elements, and arising advances. This information is essential for giving exact and applicable guidance to clients.

2. Upgrading Mastery: Ability improvement permits specialists to extend their topic skill and expand their insight across numerous spaces. By consistently working on their abilities, experts become more significant resources for their clients, offering balanced arrangements and experiences.

3. Meeting Client Assumptions: As client needs advance, persistent learning empowers advisors to meet and surpass assumptions. By developing different abilities, experts can address a more extensive scope of client challenges, prompting upgraded client fulfillment and unwaveringly.

4. Remaining Cutthroat: In an exceptionally serious consultancy scene, persistent mastering and expertise improvement give experts an upper hand. By showing their obligation to information improvement and expert development, specialists can separate themselves from their companions and draw in additional clients and open doors.

5.1.2. Systems for Execution:

1. Embrace a Learning Society: Consultancy firms ought to cultivate a culture that energizes and upholds nonstop learning. This can incorporate giving assets like preparation programs, studios, online classes, and admittance to applicable industry distributions. Laying out mentorship programs and working with information sharing meetings can likewise work with advancing inside the association.

2. Foster Customized Learning Plans: Advisors ought to be urged to make individual improvement plans custom-made to their particular requirements and objectives. These plans could distinguish ability holes and framework ventures for securing new information and capabilities. Ordinary audits and conversations with administrators can guarantee that specialists are advancing towards their learning targets.

3. Use Innovation and Online Assets: In the present computerized period, innovation assumes an urgent part in working with nonstop learning. Use internet learning stages, online courses, webcasts, and proficient organizations to furnish advisors with helpful admittance to important and cutting-edge data. Empower independent learning and influence virtual joint effort devices for information sharing and cooperative critical thinking.

4. Energize Outer Commitment: Empowering experts to take part in industry meetings, workshops, and systems administration occasions assists them with extending their expert organizations, gaining openness to thought pioneers, and remaining refreshed on the most recent industry patterns. Supporting cooperation in accreditation projects and expert affiliations can likewise improve information and validity.

Nonstop mastering and expertise improvement are basic for consultancy experts to flourish in a quickly changing business climate. By embracing a learning society, creating customized learning plans, using innovation, and empowering outer commitment, consultancy firms can guarantee that their experts stay at the front of their field. Underlining consistent mastering and ability improvement won't just drive individual development yet additionally upgrade the general mastery and seriousness of the consultancy administrations.

5.2. Accomplishing Balance Between Life Activities

Accomplishing balance between life activities for consultancy administrations can be challenging, as experts frequently manage extended periods of time, tight cutoff times, and high-pressure circumstances. Be that as it may, with cautious preparation, prioritization, and an emphasis on taking care of oneself, finding some kind of harmony among work and individual life is conceivable. In this exhaustive examination, we will investigate key procedures, advantages, and potential difficulties related with accomplishing balance between fun and serious activities with regards to consultancy administrations.

1. Using time productively: Compelling using time effectively is pivotal for keeping up with balance between fun and serious activities. Specialists ought to concentrate on arranging and setting reasonable assumptions for their responsibility. This includes booking breaks, defining limits, and keeping away from overcommitment. Using time-following devices and methods like the Pomodoro Strategy can assist with expanding efficiency while guaranteeing time for individual exercises.

2. Prioritization and Appointment: Focusing on undertakings in light of desperation and significance permits advisors to effectively apportion their time. It is crucial for delegate undertakings that can be dealt with by others, empowering advisors to zero in on high-esteem, key exercises. Compelling appointments advances work productivity, decreases pressure, and sets open doors for individual time.

3. Adaptability and Remote Work: Consultancy firms can advance balance between fun and serious activities by embracing adaptable work game plans and remote work choices when plausible. This approach permits specialists to oblige individual obligations and disposes of drive time, giving additional opportunity to individual exercises and family responsibilities.

4. Clear Correspondence and Limits: Laying out clear correspondence channels and limits with clients and colleagues is fundamental. Experts ought to impart their accessibility, reaction times, and limits forthright to deal with clients' assumptions. Transparent correspondence encourages understanding and regard, guaranteeing balance between serious and fun activities isn't compromised.

5. Taking care of oneself and Prosperity: Focusing on taking care of oneself is critical for advisors to keep up with efficiency and stay balanced. Empowering the improvement of side interests, ordinary activity, adequate rest, and a sound eating routine ought to be underlined. Associations can likewise uphold representative prosperity by giving admittance to emotional well-being assets and health programs.

By taking on these systems, experts can figure out some kind of harmony between their expert and individual lives, prompting improved prosperity and in general work fulfillment. Consultancy firms ought to likewise uphold their representatives in developing balance between serious and fun activities by executing approaches that empower adaptability, correspondence, and worker prosperity.

5.3. Leaving an Enduring Effect

Leaving an enduring effect, whether in your own life, profession, or original area, is an ideal numerous try to negotiate. It includes making a positive and persisting through effect on individualities, associations, or society overall. Then are a many vital norms and methodologies for leaving an enduring effect

Characterize Your provocation: Begin by explaining your provocation and values. Understanding the main thing to you'll direct your conditioning and choices. Knowing your "why" is vital for leaving a significant effect.

Put forth Significant objects: Lay out clear and aggressive objects that line up with your provocation. These objects ought to challenge you and propel you to have an effect.

Deep confirmed literacy: Constantly gain information and capacities. It brings about enhancement and furnishes you with the instruments to impact change and embrace development intelligence.

Credibility: Be harmonious with yourself, your validness constructs trust and believability. individualities are bound to be impacted by the people who are authentic and genuine.

Positive Impact: Develop positive connections and be a wellspring of provocation. Amp and elevate others as opposed to destroying them. Your impact ought to be a power for good.

Show others how it's done, parade the ways of carrying and esteems you believe that others should take on. Whether it's in your family, working terrain, or original area, showing others how it's done is a strong system for impacting others.

Enable Tirelessness: Comprehend that leaving an enduring effect constantly takes time and exertion. Be encouraged by mishaps or slow advancement. Remain concentrated on your objects.

Cooperation: Team up with other people who partake of your objects and values. Aggregate trials can prompt further huge and persisting influences than single undertakings.

Assess and Reflect: Routinely survey your advancement and change your procedures depending on the situation. Consider your palms and gain from your bummers.

Heritage Arranging: Consider the drawn out influence you need to leave. Heritage arranging includes meaning how your conditioning moment will shape what is to come.

Social Obligation: Perceive your job in the public arena and the obligation that accompanies it. Adding to the enhancement of your original area and the world is a strong system for leaving an enduring effect.

Lead with Sympathy: Show compassion and empathy toward others. individualities recollect how you affected them, and thoughtful gestures can have an enduring effect.

Report Your Excursion: Consider participating in your hassles and exemplifications learned through composition, talking, or different types of chronicling. Your story can motivate and direct others.

Maintainability: On the off chance that your effect includes natural or asset related issues, concentrate on manageability and aware practices to guarantee a positive heritage.

CONCLUSION

Your Future As A Prosperous Consultant

The conclusion of a book on the topic of "Wealth Strategies for Consultants" would typically sum up the key points and insights presented throughout the book, leaving readers with a sense of purpose and direction as they embark on their consulting careers. Here is a hypothetical conclusion for such a book:

In the pages of this book, we've left on an excursion to investigate the thrilling universe of consultancy and reveal the systems that can prompt success in this unique field. As we wrap up our investigation, it's fundamental to consider the key focal points that can shape your future as a prosperous expert.

Most importantly, we've stressed the significance of clearness of direction. Your consultancy profession ought to be based on an underpinning of certifiable energy and a reasonable feeling of why you've picked this way. When your "why" is solid, it will drive your activities and support your inspiration in any event, during testing times.

All through this book, we've dove into the abilities and characteristics that put effective specialists aside. From compelling correspondence and critical thinking to versatility and strength, you've seen that a balanced range of abilities is the expert's dearest companion. Persistent learning isn't simply an idea yet a prerequisite in this steadily developing field. Embrace change, and remain focused on private and expert development.

Connections are at the core of consultancy. Whether it's structure entrusted with clients, teaming up with associates, or tutoring the future, the associations you cause will be instrumental in your prosperity. Sustain these connections, for they are the structure blocks of your prosperous future.

Development has been a common topic in our conversations. Specialists are, commonly, pioneers. Embrace inventive reasoning, and seek constantly better ways of serving your clients and address their most squeezing difficulties.

As you leave on your excursion as an expert, recollect that your effect reaches out a long way past reality. Genuine thriving in consultancy isn't just about monetary achievement yet additionally about the positive and enduring impact you leave on your clients, your partners, and your local area. Be a power for good, and your success will follow.

At long last, never neglect to focus on the way that your process is extraordinarily yours. While the standards and systems framed in this book give important direction, your way to success will be an impression of your uniqueness, your encounters, and your desires. Embrace your uniqueness, and use it for your potential benefit.

With a reasonable feeling of direction, a pledge to consistent learning and development, an emphasis on building significant connections, and a steady commitment to development and good effect, your future as a prosperous specialist is splendid and loaded with potential.

As you close this book and forward-moving step into your consultancy profession, realize that you have the information, the abilities, and the mentality to flourish. The universe of consultancy is sitting tight for your exceptional commitments. Do something significant, leave an enduring heritage, and flourish in a literal sense.

Congrats on your excursion ahead, and may it be loaded up with success, satisfaction, and the acknowledgment of your most aggressive dreams.

This end embodies the center standards and messages of the book, leaving perusers roused and prepared to embrace their future as prosperous specialists.

www.ingramcontent.com/pod-product-compliance
Lightning Source LLC
Chambersburg PA
CBHW062330290526
45794CB00005B/1974